Happy Cooking

—

[illegible]

Ferry Project

Celebrating 25 Years

THE FOUR SEASONS

ALISON CROUCH

Ferry Project

The Four Seasons

Cover and interior design by Liz Carter

Hardback ISBN: 978-1-0683327-1-5

First published in 2024 by Ferry Project, 10a-14 South Brink, Wisbech, PE13 1JQ, United Kingdom.

www.ferryproject.org.uk

Registered Charity No. 1075389

Company No. 03742477

Contents

Introduction

Hello and welcome to The Four Seasons, our cookbook celebrating The Ferry Project's 25th anniversary.

The Ferry Project is a homelessness charity based in Fenland, in the UK. We provide a home and loving support for homeless people across the Fens, ensuring each person is seen as an individual and knows that they are valuable and worthwhile. Together with our clients we help them walk away from homelessness and into independence and hope.

We've introduced each season in this book with a short section which gives you a glimpse into the Ferry Project's journey over the past 25 years as well as share some stories from a few of the thousands of people we have helped.

Within these pages you'll find 10 delicious recipes for each season that use ingredients you'll find easily at that time of year. The recipes have come from an array of events that we run across the region in the community and at Octavia View. These include Pop Up Restaurants, Cook and Go Sessions, Afternoon Teas, Lecture Lunches, Cookery Demos and Talks plus much more. These events help to bring in revenue to help sustain the cookery classes we run with our clients.

By buying this book, you'll not only learn to make tasty food, but you're also supporting the important work of the Ferry Project, helping us to continue our work with the homeless in the Fenland area.

I hope that this book inspires you, both with cooking and with knowing there is hope for the homeless, if they are given the love and support they need.

Thank you, and happy cooking,

Alison

wi

nter

Before the Ferry Project

Wisbech is a market town with a rich history. Sitting in the heart of the Fens, it once boasted a bustling port and thriving economy. However, the train line closed in 1968, taking most of the high paid jobs with it, and by the 1990s Wisbech had become a small town off the beaten track with agriculture as its main trade. The town was no longer booming, and there wasn't much to draw people in.

However, there was one group of people who would regularly come to town. Agricultural workers. Throughout the year these people drifted into Wisbech looking for seasonal work.

Sadly, not everyone found the opportunities they hoped for. Instead, some found themselves living on the streets with no income and no home.

At the same time, a number of teenagers were leaving struggling homes in a bid to find freedom and opportunity. But the burden of sudden responsibility weighed heavy, leaving many of these young people homeless.

Wisbech was also home to a number of ex-armed forces personnel, people who bravely served their country yet became unable to work, often due to their physical and mental health. Many of them also found themselves without a home.

Meanwhile, there was no legal obligation for the local authority to help these people. Homelessness had become a difficult and very visible problem for Wisbech.

Seeing the need, the local churches began to help. Soon they were offering financial aid and hosting people in their homes. They quickly learned that the homeless needed a lot of support and care, more than many of the host families were able to give. However, they also saw firsthand the amazing impact that a loving home could have.

It was clear that a more robust support system was needed. Wisbech Churches Together then banded together to create a charity dedicated to not only providing a home for the homeless, but also supporting them with love on their individual journey to independence.

Thus, in 1999, the Ferry Project was born.

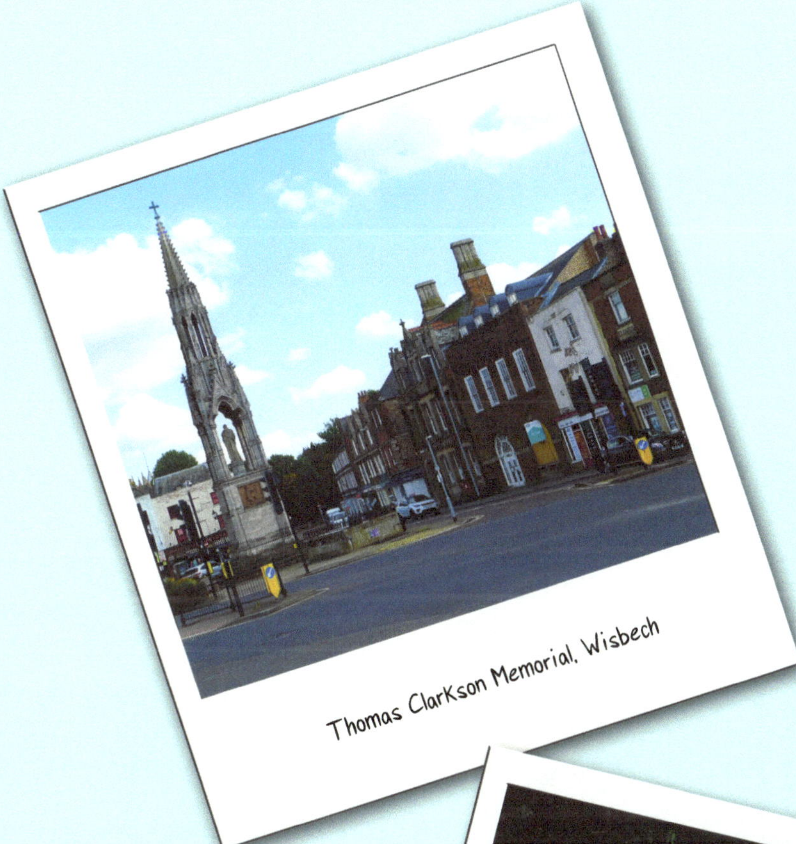

Thomas Clarkson Memorial, Wisbech

Rough sleeping near farmer's field

A Ferry Project client

William's* Story

I was in my thirties, married with three kids, looking after my wife who has some physical needs. We were getting by. That's when my dad died of lung disease. It devastated me. My mum moved on really quickly and married someone else, and our relationship collapsed.

It was all too much. I got really depressed, especially after finding out I had COPD, the disease my dad died of. I hit rock bottom, was having panic attacks all the time, and the only thing that helped was booze. I wasted all our money on getting drunk, and my wife couldn't take it anymore. She kicked me out.

I was all alone, in debt, and I'd spend my nights writing suicide notes because my anxiety wouldn't let me sleep. That's when I found the Ferry Project.

They took me in and listened to me. They had hope that my life would improve, even though I didn't. But they were right.

They introduced me to a mental health team, and I began to open up to them about everything. I went to grief counselling and finally came to terms with my dad's death, and faced the fears I had of dying the same way.

I started getting better. The Ferry Project helped me to get benefits, and I began paying off my debt. I joined a gym, and started helping out around the hostel. I even cooked the Sunday roast each week.

At last I started to believe in myself again, just as Ferry had believed in me all along.

When the time was right, I reached out to my family and asked for their forgiveness. I was amazed when my wife told me I could come home! After six months at the Ferry Project I returned to my wife and my kids, ready to restore our relationships.

It was a long road, but there's no chance I would've made it without the Ferry Project. I'm so glad I'm still alive today, and back with the people I love the most.

*Name changed

Brussel Sprout and Cheddar Soup

25g butter • 1 tbsp rapeseed oil • 1 red onion, peeled and diced • 2 cloves garlic, crushed • 1 cm root ginger, finely diced • 700g Brussel Sprouts, trimmed • 700ml vegetable stock • A handful thyme • 100g cheddar, grated • Salt and pepper • 50ml cream

Melt the butter in a saucepan with the oil. Add the onion, garlic and ginger. Fry for 5 minutes on a medium heat or until the onion is softening.

Add the sprouts. Fry for a few minutes, stirring well. Add the stock and thyme. Simmer, with a lid on for 25 minutes.

Blitz with a handheld blender or food processor until smooth. Add in the cheese. Stir well until melted.

Add the cream and season to taste.

Adjust with a little water if needed.

Walnut and Goats Cheese Fougasse

225g white bread flour • ½ tsp salt • 10g fresh yeast • 110ml water, lukewarm • 1 tsp olive oil

FILLING:

75g goats cheese • 25g chopped walnuts • 1 tbsp honey

Lightly grease a baking sheet.

In a bowl sieve together the flour and salt. In a jug mix together the yeast, water and oil. Pour into the flour and form a dough.

Knead on a floured surface for 10 minutes. Place a little oil into the bowl. Place the dough into the bowl and cover, leave to rise for 1 hour.

Knock back and roll the dough into a large oval. Dot with the cheese and sprinkle with walnuts. Drizzle with honey. Fold the bottom third up to the middle and the top third over the top. Roll out and refold as before, roll out again and repeat twice more.

Cut three diagonal slashes across the middle and gently stretch the dough to form slashes in the dough. Place on the baking sheet and leave to rise for 30 minutes.

Preheat the oven to 220C/200C Fan/ Gas Mark 7. Brush the bread with a little oil and bake for 25 minutes or until golden and risen.

Leek, Bacon and Binham Blue Tart

PASTRY:

175g plain flour • 75g salted butter • A sprinkling of fresh thyme

FILLING:

1 tbsp rapeseed oil • 25g butter • 2 rashers smoked bacon, cut into small pieces • 2 leeks, washed and sliced • 2 cloves garlic, crushed • Salt and pepper • 200g cream cheese • 175ml double cream • 4 eggs • 50g cheddar, grated • 100g binham blue, crumbled

Make the pastry. Sieve the flour. Rub in the butter. Add in the thyme. Form into a dough with a little cold water. Cover and place in the fridge for 20 minutes.

Make the filling: Place the oil and butter in a pan. Turn to a medium heat. Fry the bacon, leeks and garlic for about 8 minutes on a low heat to really soften the leeks. Season well. Place to one side.

Roll out the pastry and line a 20cm deep flan tin. Bake blind for 20 minutes at 190C, 170C Fan, Gas Mark 5.

Reduce the heat of the oven to 160C, 140C Fan, Gas Mark 3.

Beat together the cream cheese, double cream and eggs. Stir in the cheeses.

Place the bacon, leeks and garlic in the pastry case. Pour on the cheese mixture. Bake for 30 to 40 minutes or until set.

You can leave the bacon out for a vegetarian version.

Spaghetti with Steak and Red Wine

200g spaghetti • 1 red onion, diced • 1 clove garlic, crushed • 2 tbsp olive oil • 2 steaks cut into strips • 100ml red wine • 1 tin chopped tomatoes • A good handful of basil • Salt and pepper

Bring a pan of water to the boil. Add the spaghetti and stir. Simmer for 8 to 10 minutes.

Fry the onion and garlic in the oil for 3 minutes. Add in the steak and fry for 2 to 3 minutes on a medium heat. Stir in the red wine and tinned tomatoes. Add a ladle of spaghetti water.

Simmer for 3 to 4 minutes. Drain the spaghetti and stir in. Add the basil. Season well and serve.

Fish Pie

TOPPING:

500g potatoes • 25g butter • 25ml milk •
Salt and pepper

FILLING:

150ml full fat milk • 340g fish pie mix • 160g raw prawns • 200g tin crabmeat • 30g butter • 30g plain flour • 100ml fish stock • 50ml white wine • 150g ricotta • 2 tsp dried tarragon • 50ml double cream • 50g peas • Salt and Pepper

Peel and chop the potatoes and put in a pan. Cover with water and bring to the boil. Simmer for 10 to 15 minutes or until soft when a knife is inserted. Drain and then mash with the butter and milk. Season to taste. Put to one side.

Put the fish in a saucepan with the milk. Simmer for 8 minutes. Remove the fish from the pan and place into an oven proof dish. Add the prawns on top. Sprinkle on the crabmeat.

Pour the milk from the pan into a jug.

Wipe out the pan. Place back on a low heat. Add the butter and melt. Add the flour.

Take off the heat and gradually add the milk a little at a time. Stir well until all the milk is incorporated. Add the fish stock and wine. Place back on the heat and bring to the boil until bubbling and thickened. Stir in the ricotta, tarragon and cream. Mix in the peas. Season to taste.

Pour over the fish and top with the potatoes.

Bake at 190C/170C Fan/Gas Mark 5 for 25 to 30 minutes until golden and bubbling.

Mushroom Plait

1 tbsp olive oil • 25g butter • 1 clove garlic, crushed • 1 onion, diced • 1 stick celery, sliced • 125g chestnut mushrooms, cleaned and quartered • 125g oyster mushrooms, cleaned, halved, quartered • 125g shiitake mushrooms • 100ml vegetable stock • 2 dessert spoons PX sherry • Salt and black pepper • 50ml crème fraiche • 2 tsp dried tarragon • 1 packet puff pastry • 1 tbsp milk for glazing

Heat a large saucepan. Add the oil and butter, add the garlic and onion and fry for 5 minutes, stirring, until soft. Add the celery and mushrooms. Fry for a few minutes until cooked through.

Add the stock and sherry and season with salt and pepper. Simmer for 5 minutes. Add the crème fraiche and tarragon. Season to taste then set aside to cool.

Heat the oven to 200C/Fan 180C/Gas Mark 6.

Meanwhile, roll the pastry into a rectangle. Make short diagonal cuts to form strips on either side, but leaving a section down the middle for the filling, that will reach across the width of the pastry.

Place the mushroom mixture down the middle. Lift the strips over the pastry at an angle alternating to form a plait.

Brush with a little milk.

Bake for 15 minutes at 200C, then turn the oven to 160C/140C/Gas Mark 3 for 15 minutes. The plait should be golden on top. Serve warm or at room temperature.

Beer Braised Vegetable Pie

1 onion, diced • 1 celery stick, washed and sliced • 1 clove garlic, crushed • 25g butter • 25g flour • 1 kilo (after peeling) – carrots, parsnips, swede, cauliflower, diced • 500ml beer • 2 vegetable stock cubes • 2 sprigs thyme

PASTRY:

50g butter • 175g plain flour • 125g mashed potato • Salt and pepper • 1 egg, beaten

Heat oven to 160C,140C fan, Gas Mark 3. Using a flameproof casserole dish with a lid, soften the onion, celery and garlic in the butter. Stir in the flour until it has disappeared, then stir in the vegetables and beer. Crumble in stock cubes and add thyme. Pour over the ale, bring to a simmer, then cover and cook in the oven for 35mins. Remove lid and cook for another 30 mins – this should result in a thickened sauce.

Increase oven to 200C,180C fan, Gas Mark 6.

Rub the 50g butter into the 175g flour. Add the mash. Season well. Form into a dough. Add a little milk if too dry.

Roll out the pastry and lift it onto the vegetables. Tuck the edge down the sides of the dish and the vegetables. Brush the top of the pie and with beaten egg. Bake for 30-35 mins until golden brown and crisp.

Chocolate and Cranberry Roulade

200g plain chocolate • 5 eggs • 150g caster sugar • 150ml double cream • 150g fresh or frozen cranberries • 1 orange, zest and juice • 50g caster sugar • Grand marnier (optional) • 100g dark chocolate for decorating

Line a swiss roll tin with baking parchment. Preheat the oven to 200C,180C Fan, Gas Mark 6. Put the chocolate into a bain marie. Melt gently. Separate the eggs. Beat the yolks with the caster sugar until pale. Whisk the egg whites. Add the melted chocolate to the egg yolk mixture. Fold in the egg whites with a metal spoon. Bake for 10-12 minutes until firm to touch.

Slide the cake on it's parchment out of the tin onto a rack. Cover with a teatowel and leave to cool.

Prepare the cranberries. In a pan place the cranberries, orange zest and juice. Add the sugar, slowly warm through to dissolve the sugar. Simmer on a low heat for 10 -15 minutes or until the cranberries are soft. Stir in the liqueur if using.

Turn the roulade upside down onto a piece of greaseproof which has been sprinkled with caster sugar. Whip the cream. Spread on the roulade. Top with the cranberries. Roll up gently. Place onto a long plate. Remove the parchment. It will crack!

Place in the fridge. Melt the chocolate and flick over the roulade. You could make swirls on parchment. Once set use some of the cream to dot across the top, place the swirls on top and a few cranberries.

Ginger Trifle

200g ginger sponge cake • 4 tbsp apricot jam • 200g amaretti biscuits, save a few for decorating. • 100ml orange juice • 1 jar stem ginger • 2 oranges plus one for decoration • 250ml Mascarpone • 300ml Double cream • 100g icing sugar

Tear up the ginger sponge and lay in the base of a trifle dish.

Roughly spread on the apricot jam. Crumble the amaretti biscuits over the top. Pour over the orange juice. Drizzle 2 tbsp stem ginger juice over the top. Leave to soak.

Segment the oranges. Catch any juice and pour over the sponge.

Place the orange segments on top of the biscuits.

Whip the mascarpone with the cream. Fold in the icing sugar.

Place on the top of the trifle.

Decorate with sliced stem ginger, amaretti biscuits and segmented oranges. For a boozy version add a splash of brandy into the cream mixture and drizzle ginger wine over the ginger cake to soak into the sponge.

Orange And Marzipan Cake

225g butter • 225g caster sugar • 4 eggs, separated yolks from whites • 225g self raising flour • 100g marzipan grated • 100g marzipan, diced • 2 oranges • 50g icing sugar

Grease and line an 18cm (7inch) round cake tin. Turn oven to 160C, 140C Fan, Gas Mark 3

Cream together the butter and sugar. Beat in the egg yolks. Fold in the flour and the marzipan, grated and diced. Add the zest and juice of the oranges. Whisk the egg whites and fold in. Pour into the tin and bake for 30 – 35 minutes or until a skewer comes out clean.

Cool then dredge with icing sugar. Delicious with a dollop of clotted cream or crème fraiche.

sp

ring

Ferry Project's beginnings and early growth

At the turn of the millennium, there was new hope for Wisbech's homeless residents. The Ferry Project opened in 1999, with the support of local churches and the Oasis Charitable Trust. A young couple offered to be the first 'house parents', living with and caring for a homeless person. Equipped with knowledge, love, a few rented rooms and £300 raised from church donations, we took in our first client; a local teenage boy who at long last began his journey towards independence.

Meanwhile, we sought more accommodation to allow us to support more than one person. However, every time a rental agency learned what the homes would be used for, they turned us down.

A couple from The King's Church then made us an offer; rent their house while they moved elsewhere. Their incredible generosity allowed us to now care for up to three residents at a time.

In the early 2000s, we were also blessed with a Fundraiser who raised £100,000 for the Ferry Project. We could now buy a three bedroom house, and pay our 'house parents'.

From this point, things began to snowball. We rented another three bedroom house, developed a 24 hour support model, involved the local authority in our work, and built strong relationships with local lettings agencies, which meant that when the time was right our clients could move on into affordable local accommodation.

Then, in 2003, we received the Supporting People grant. At this point, everything changed. Our turnover increased massively, allowing us to hire more staff members while renting and purchasing more properties, including an entire block of flats.

We found ourselves caring for dozens of clients at any one time, with 50% of them moving on successfully.

In 2009, we purchased Octavia View, a beautiful Grade II* listed building on Wisbech's striking riverfront, which acts as our main site, and a community hub, to this day.

In ten years, the Ferry Project had blossomed into a fully-fledged charity impacting hundreds of lives every year.

Tinkers Drove, where it all began

Keith Smith in the early years

Anton's* Story

I was born in Poland and moved to the UK searching for new opportunities, but it didn't go as I'd planned. The pandemic hit and I ended up homeless, living in a tent. One day, I came back and saw that someone had set fire to my tent. Everything I owned was in there, even my passport and my immigration documents. I had nothing.

I didn't have settled status yet, so I wasn't allowed to live in the UK permanently, but I had no way to get back home. I'm very dyslexic, so learning English was really tough, and I could hardly read and write in Polish. I was so lost.

Then I found the Ferry Project.

I was so anxious, but slowly I learned to trust these people. Before long I moved into their emergency accommodation, Destiny Haven.

The wonderful people at Ferry helped me to finish my immigration application, and I was granted settled status! This meant I could apply for Universal Credit, so I finally had some money coming in.

Ferry gave me a Polish key worker who helped me to fill out forms, apply for benefits, make appointments, and they even helped me to chat with the mental health nurse.

It was a hard journey. My anxiety made life really difficult, and I didn't trust doctors and nurses. My case worker came with me to my appointments. I was terrified when they told me I needed to have a blood test, I can't cope with needles! But with Ferry's help I got through it.

In time I found a good rhythm, and the Ferry team taught me how to budget my money so that I could stick to my payment plans. I now live debt free in Jubilee Place, Ferry's move-on accommodation, where I am preparing to live independently.

After a few awful years, I finally have a home, I have friends, and I have hope again.

*Name changed

Sleeping rough

Pea and Mint Soup

(Based on a Cambridgeshire recipe from the 1800s)

3 onions • 1 clove garlic, crushed • 25g butter •
1 lettuce, washed • 2 large potatoes, peeled and diced •
450g peas, fresh or frozen • 450ml vegetable stock •
1 tbsp each of a variety of herbs such as parsley, sorrel,
mint… • 150ml cream • Salt and pepper

Dice the onions. Put them in a pan with the garlic and butter. Fry until soft. Shred the lettuce and add to the pan with the potatoes. Add the peas and the stock. Cook gently until the peas and potatoes are tender.

Add the herbs, then blend the soup and stir in the cream. Season to taste.

Cheese Scones

Makes 10 to 12 scones

800g self raising flour • 300g butter • 275g cheddar, grated • 375ml full fat milk • Milk to glaze

Turn oven to 200C Fan 180C Gas 6.

Sieve the flour into a bowl. Rub in the butter. Stir in most of the cheese. Save a little for the scone tops. Stir in the milk and form a dough.

Turn onto a floured surface. Knead gently for a minute or two to form a smooth dough. Flatten with your hand to about 2cm thick and circular in shape. Ensure a consistent thickness across the dough.

Cut into circles with a medium sized cutter Place on a baking tray. Brush with milk. Top with reserved cheese.

Bake for approximately 25 to 30 minutes until risen and golden.

Meatball Ragu with Tagliatelle and a Parmesan Crisp

40g white bread (no crusts) • 2 tbsp milk • 200g beef mince • 200g pork mince • 2 cloves garlic • ½ red chilli • ½ tsp cumin • ½ tsp ground coriander • 1 tsp paprika • 2 tbsp parsley • Salt and pepper • 2 tbsp olive oil

SAUCE:

200ml red wine • 2 cloves garlic • ½ red onion • 1 tin chopped tomatoes • Pinch of sugar • 2tsp paprika • Parsley to serve

Tagliatelle: 400g • Parmesan Crisp – 80g parmesan

Put the bread in a bowl and add the milk. Soak for 5 minutes. Add the mince, crushed garlic, finely diced chilli, spices, chopped parsley and seasoning.

Mix well and form into small meatballs (about 16). Heat the olive oil and fry until browned all over on a medium heat.

Remove from the pan. Put to one side. Pour the red wine into the pan with the crushed garlic and finely diced onion. Bring to the boil and reduce. Add the tin of tomatoes and paprika. Simmer for 10 minutes, then add the meatballs back in.

Simmer for a further 20 minutes until the sauce is thickened and the meatballs are cooked through.

Cook the tagliatelle by bringing a pan of water to the boil with a spoonful of olive oil. Gently drop the tagliatelle in and simmer for 8 minutes. Serve the meatballs on nests of tagliatelle topped with the parmesan crisp and sprinkled with parsley.

For the crisps grate the parmesan and form 4 piles on a grill pan. Place under the grill until melted, bubbling and turning golden.

Paneer and Caramelised Red Onion Hummus Flatbreads

200g Paneer • 1 tbsp oil • 1 cm root ginger, grated • 2 clove garlic, crushed • Pinch of chilli flakes • 2 tsp cumin • 25g butter • 100g sprouting broccoli, sliced • 50g peas • Salt and pepper • 2 flatbreads

HUMMUS:

2 red onions • 25g butter • 1 tbsp oil • Salt • 1 tin chickpeas • 1 tbsp tahini

Start with the hummus: Slice the onion and fry in the butter and oil on a low heat with a pinch of salt until soft and caramelised. This will take approximately 30 to 40 minutes.

Meanwhile dice the paneer into 1cm cubes. Place in a bowl with the oil, root ginger, garlic, chilli flakes and cumin. Leave for 30 minutes.

In a pan melt the butter. Add the broccoli. Stir fry for a few minutes until beginning to soften. Add the paneer and spices. Fry for a few minutes. Add in the peas. Season well.

In a blender put the chickpeas and tahini paste with ¾ of the red onion. Blitz until smooth – add a little oil to slacken if needed. Season to taste. Warm the flatbreads in the grill.

Spread the hummus onto the flatbreads. Top with the paneer mixture. Then spoon on the remaining caramelised onions.

Asparagus and Pancetta Risotto

1 litre vegetable stock • 500g of asparagus • 150g of pancetta • Vegetable oil, for frying • 2 onions, diced • 3 garlic cloves, crushed. • 300g of carnaroli risotto rice, or arborio rice • 200ml of white wine • 50g of butter • 60g of parmesan, grated • 1 lemon, zested and juiced • Sea salt • Pepper

Put the stock in a pan and simmer with the asparagus until softened, then lift out the asparagus. Slice into 1 cm pieces. Put to one side.

Fry the pancetta for 2 minutes in the oil, stirring. Add the onion and garlic. Fry for 3 minutes, until softened. Add the rice and stir well. Add the wine. Let the rice absorb the wine.

Add ladles of warm stock one by one, each time letting the rice absorb the stock before adding the next. Stir regularly to release the starch from the rice, which is what gives you a creamy risotto.

Once the stock is absorbed stir in the asparagus pieces. Save a few to garnish.

Stir in the butter and Parmesan. Add the lemon juice and zest. Season to taste.

Serve with the saved asparagus on top to garnish.

For a vegetarian version leave out the pancetta and add peas, courgettes or mushrooms. (Or all!)

Teriyaki Chicken Pittas – Fiery Food for Outdoors

This can be cooked over a fire pit or BBQ and is delicious as a warming outdoor dish! The dish was invented for the Outdoor Cooking on the Market Place events.

SAUCE:

300ml water • 50g brown sugar • 50ml dark soy sauce • 2 tbsp honey • 2 garlic cloves, crushed • 2 cm root ginger, grated • 1 tbsp rice wine vinegar • 1 tbsp cornflour

4 chicken breasts, diced • 2 tbsp rapeseed oil • 2 spring onions, chopped • ½ red pepper, chopped • Shredded lettuce • 4 pitta breads

Put the water in a pan with the sugar. Bring to the boil to dissolve the sugar. Add the Soy sauce, honey, garlic and ginger. Simmer for several minutes to reduce the sauce so it becomes slightly thicker. Add the rice wine vinegar. Place the cornflour in a bowl, stir in a tbsp water and stir into the sauce, bring to the boil. It will thicken. Taste and adjust with a little vinegar if required.

Stir fry the chicken in a little oil for about 5 minutes. Add in the chopped spring onions and red pepper. Fry for 2 minutes. Add the sauce and simmer for 5 minutes.

Open up the pittas, place in the shredded lettuce and spoon in the chicken mixture. Eat!

Nutty Rhubarb Crumble Cake with Thunder and Lightning

3 sticks rhubarb • 2 tbsp caster sugar • 125g butter • 125g caster sugar • 2 eggs • 125g self-raising flour • 1 tsp Vanilla extract

TOPPING:

125g plain flour • 50g butter • 50g demerara sugar • 25g chopped hazelnuts • 25g chopped almonds • 1 tsp cinnamon

TO SERVE:

300ml clotted cream • 2 tbsp golden syrup • 2 tsp black treacle • 1 tsp cinnamon for dusting

Turn oven to 180C/160 Fan/Gas Mark 4

Chop the rhubarb and place in a pan with 2 tbsp water and the caster sugar. Gently cook until the rhubarb is soft.

Cream the butter and sugar. Fold in the eggs. Sieve in the flour. Fold in the extract. Place in a greased square cake tin or ovenproof dish.

Make the crumble topping by rubbing the butter into the flour. Stir in the sugar, nuts and cinnamon.

Cool the rhubarb slightly and spoon onto the sponge. Sprinkle over the crumble.

Bake for 35 to 40 minutes until firm to touch. Serve hot or cold but delicious warm with Thunder and Lightning, or custard!

For the Thunder and Lightning: Whip the cream and gently incorporate the syrup, black treacle and cinnamon.

UN MONDO DI VINO!!!
Grappa Vin Santo Chianti
Chianti Nobile
STORK
PYREX

Lemon and Blueberry Cake with Mascarpone

CAKE:

225g butter • 225g caster sugar • 4 eggs • 225g self raising flour • Rind of 2 lemons

BLUEBERRY SYRUP:

75g blueberries • 25g caster sugar • ½ tsp vanilla essence • 1 tbsp water

ICING:

100ml double cream • 1 tub mascarpone • Juice of 2 lemons • 150g icing sugar

Make the cake: heat the oven to 180C/ Fan 160C/Gas Mark 4. Grease and line two sandwich tins.

Cream together the butter and sugar. Fold in the eggs. Sieve the flour and fold in with the lemon rind.

Split into the tins and bake for 20 to 25 minutes until firm to touch. Leave in the tins to settle then turn out and cool.

Make the blueberry syrup – In a small pan place the blueberries, sugar, vanilla essence and water. Slowly bring to the boil and simmer for 3 to 5 minutes until it is slightly thick and syrupy. Put to one side to cool.

Icing: With an electric whisk beat together the double cream, mascarpone, lemon juice and icing sugar until thick.

Once the cake has cooled spread half of the icing onto the base sponge. Spread one third of the blueberry syrup onto the icing. Place the other sponge on top. Spread with the remaining icing. Drizzle the rest of the blueberry syrup over the top and swirl into the icing.

Enjoy with lashings of tea!

THE GREAT
STAND
UP TO
CANCER
BAKE OFF
STORK
STORK

Earl Grey Tea Loaf

200g sultanas • Juice and zest of 1 orange • 175ml Earl Grey Tea, hot • 25ml brandy • 1 tbsp honey • 175g self raising flour • 50g butter • 75g caster sugar

Turn the oven to 180C/160C/Gas Mark 3. Grease and line a 450g loaf tin.

Place the sultanas in a bowl with the zest and juice of an orange. Pour over the hot tea and add the brandy. Add the honey. Stir well and leave to stand for an hour.

In a bowl sieve the flour. Rub in the butter. Stir in the sugar.

Pour in the tea mixture and stir well. Pour into the loaf tin and bake for 35 minutes or until firm to touch.

Remove from the oven and leave to cool. Serve sliced with butter.

Marmalade Cake with Clotted Cream

150g butter • 175g caster sugar • 3 eggs • 150g self raising flour • 75g ground almonds • 50g clotted cream • 2 tbsp marmalade

DRIZZLE:

50g icing sugar • 2 tbsp marmalade • Zest and juice of 1 orange • Clotted cream to serve

Preheat the oven to 180°C/Fan 160°C? Gas Mark 4. Grease an 18cm round cake tin and line the base with baking paper.

Cream together the butter and caster sugar. Fold in the eggs, self-raising flour, and ground almonds until combined. Stir in the cream. Swirl through the marmalade. Spoon into the prepared tin, smooth the top and bake for 40 to 45 minutes.

For the drizzle beat together the icing sugar with the marmalade, orange zest and juice until the sugar has dissolved.

As soon as the cake comes out of the oven, prick all over the top with a skewer and spoon over the marmalade syrup. Leave to cool in the tin before serving.

Serve warm with clotted cream. Or leave to cool and enjoy a slice with your coffee.

BREAD

sum

mer

Ferry Project now: current services and statistics

In 2024, the Ferry Project celebrated its 25th anniversary. Events across Wisbech celebrated the thousands of people no longer homeless because of the love and care of so many, both within the Ferry Project, and further afield through our partners and supporters.

Not only was this a year of jubilation, but also one of reaping the fruit of 25 years of dedicated service whilst seeing even more abundant growth.

We were now able to house 82 clients across Fenland at any one time, not just by providing much-needed homes, but developing individual support plans for each and every client, ensuring their individual needs were heard and met on a holistic level.

To achieve this, we developed a number of different places to stay, whether for those simply in need of a comfy bed and a warm shower, to women needing a haven from domestic abuse, to those learning the skills needed to successfully live on their own. With over 40 staff, we could show care and love in every facet of the charity 24/7, 365 days a year. This led to 95% of our clients moving on successfully from our service, or into other supported accommodation, between 2023 and 2024.

We hosted many celebrations in The Queen Mary Centre, a community space which we saved from demolition and now manage. By 2024, over 70,000 people were visiting the centre every year, many of whom were finding love, support and skills to help them to never reach homelessness, even in the toughest times.

Octavia View is now thriving. The Ferry Project Cookery School has adapted our kitchens, creating a cutting-edge space to provide valuable cooking skills to our clients whilst offering high quality classes and events for anybody who wants to learn more about preparing delicious food.

Meanwhile, the Wisbech Gallery displays artwork from both local and international artists for our clients and the public to enjoy. We now have a place where anyone could retreat and ponder the world around us through the lens of creativity and inspiration.

People are at the heart of what we do. All we have achieved in 25 years is thanks to countless dedicated staff members, dozens of volunteers, hundreds of generous donors, and the commitment of our clients to seek a better life, one filled with hope and the promise of a new, brighter day.

Octavia View

Destiny Haven

Vicky's* Story

I was with my partner for many years. It was a difficult relationship, and in 2022 they diagnosed me with bipolar disorder. I got really ill, and they sectioned me for six weeks. While I was in care, the doctors found out about my abusive partner. They told me to end the relationship, so I did.

When I left the psychiatric ward, he didn't let me back into my home. Because I'd been in care, he was now in charge of my finances, and he didn't give control back to me. I had no home and no money, so I ended up on the streets.

I was desperate for help, and a local support team got me housed in a hostel and helped me to get support from a mental health team.

Then in January 2023 I got my own accommodation through the Next Steps Accommodation Programme, who work with the Ferry Project to help get homeless people back on their feet.

The Ferry Project was brilliant. They were on my side from day one, and they helped me to get back control of my finances! They visited me every week, helping me to budget my money and stay on top of my rent.

I always looked forward to their visits. They would always say how clean and comfortable my home was. Since leaving my ex-partner, I know what a difference it makes for your home to be a safe haven.

Without the Ferry Project's constant support, I would've never coped with taking back control of my life. But now I'm thriving. I volunteer at the local charity shop, play tennis, swim and I'm even learning to play the guitar. It's been a rough journey, but it was worth fighting for the life I have today.

*Name changed

A Ferry Project client

Roasted Red Pepper Soup

5 red peppers • 1 onion • 2 carrots • 2 garlic cloves • 4 tbsp rapeseed oil • 1 large potato • 500ml vegetable stock • ½ tbsp harissa paste • Handful fresh basil • 1 tsp dried oregano • 50ml double cream • Salt and pepper

Halve and take out the middle of the peppers. Roughly chop the onion and carrots. Place all in a baking tray with the garlic cloves. Drizzle with the oil. Season. Roast at 180C/160 Fan/Gas mark 4 for approximately 25 minutes until soft. Pull off any skin from the peppers that you can.

Place into a pan. Peel and chop the potatoes and add to the pan with the roasted vegetables. Add the stock and paste. Simmer for 30 minutes. Add the basil and oregano.

Blend until smooth. Stir in the double cream. Season to taste.

Mushroom Focaccia

150g strong white bread flour • 200g spelt flour • Pinch of salt • 1 sachet or 1 heaped tsp dried yeast • 1 tbsp olive oil • 6 flat mushrooms, peeled with the stalk left in • 25g butter • 25g parmesan • 2 cloves garlic, crushed • A handful of fresh thyme • Sea salt • 2 tbsp olive oil

Preheat the oven to 200C / 180C fan or Gas Mark 6.

Place both the flours in a bowl with the salt. Stir the yeast into 175ml warm water. Add the 1 tbsp oil. Pour into the flour and form into a dough. Knead for 10 minutes. Put to one side to rise.

Prepare the mushrooms by frying in the butter until softened. Put to one side.

After 1 hour knock back the dough. Grease a baking sheet or Swiss Roll tin and push the dough into the tin to flatten. Leave to rise for 10 minutes. Push the mushrooms, stalk side up into the dough. Sprinkle on the parmesan, garlic, thyme and salt. Drizzle over any butter left in the pan and the oil. Leave for ten minutes.

Bake for about 25 to 30 minutes until golden.

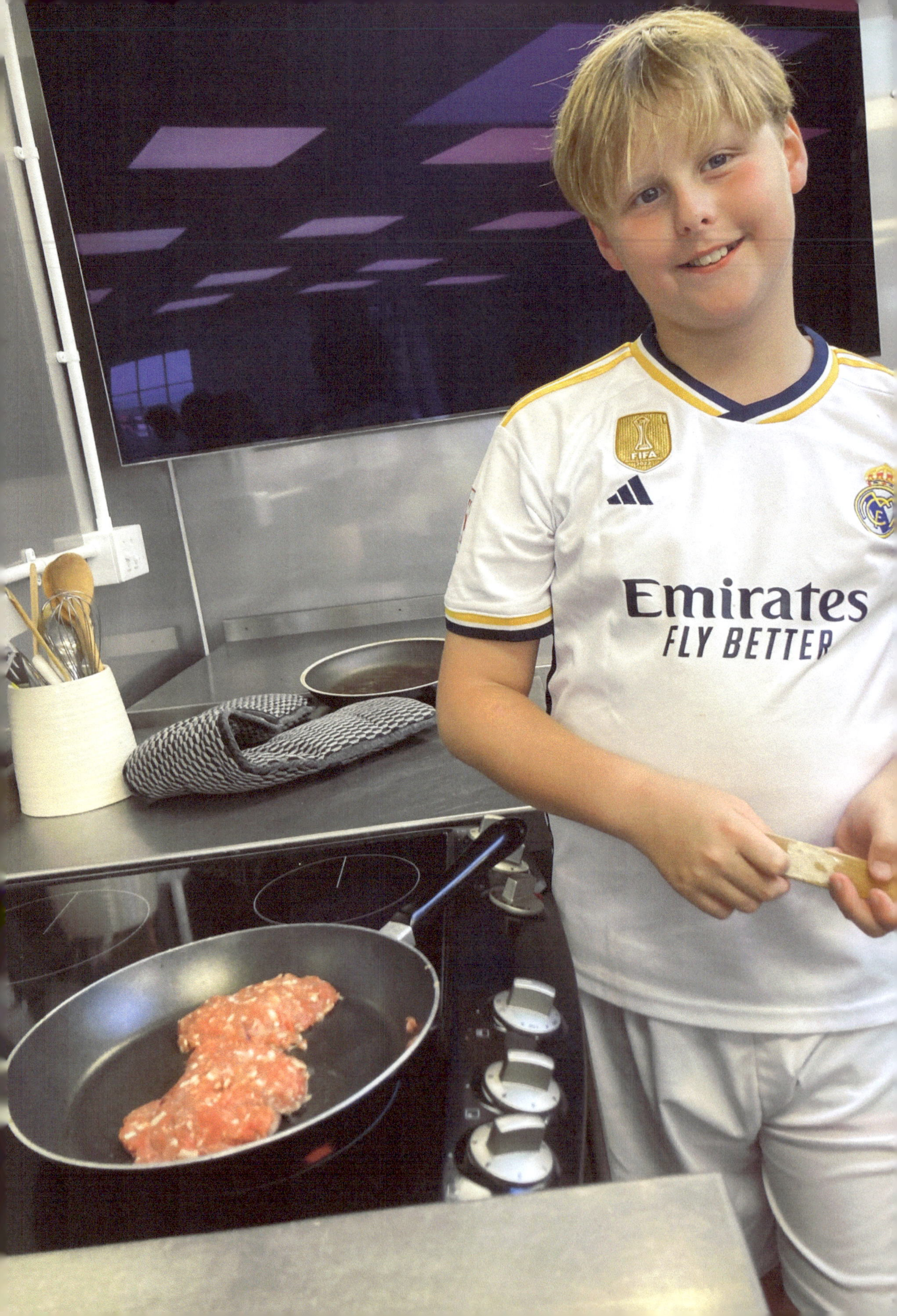
Emirates
FLY BETTER

Courgette Ribbons with Courgette Flowers, Walnuts and Stilton

2 cloves garlic, crushed • 2 tbsp olive oil • Juice and zest of 1 lemon • 4 courgettes, in ribbons – use a straight sided peeler to form the ribbons • 75g walnuts roughly chopped • 25g pinenuts • 75g blue cheese • 8 courgette flowers - petals, wiped and cut into strips • 2 Chive flowers, with the petals pulled (opt)

Fry the garlic in the oil on a low heat to avoid burning, add in the lemon juice and zest. Add in the courgettes, and fry, stirring until they begin to soften. Stir through the walnuts, pinenuts and chopped blue cheese. Pan fry until the cheese is just beginning to melt. Stir in the courgette petals, cook for one minute. Serve as a starter or a side dish for a BBQ.

Spicy Prawn Skewers with Chapatis

MARINADE:

2 tbsp oil • 2 cloves garlic crushed • Juice and rind of 1 lemon • 1 cm root ginger, grated

300g prawns, raw • 1 clove garlic • 1 cm root ginger • 2 spring onions • 1 red pepper • ½ red chilli • 2 tbsp oil • 2 tsp garam masala • 3 tbsp water • Salt and pepper • A handful of chopped coriander • 6 dessertspoons natural yoghurt • 2 tbsp Mango chutney • 4 chapatis or two naan breads • 4 kebab sticks (if wooden soak before using)

Make the marinade by mixing all the ingredients together. Stir in the prawns. Cover and leave in the fridge for 1 hour.

Crush the garlic. Finely dice the ginger. Slice the spring onions. Dice the red pepper. Dice the chilli. Fry the garlic, ginger and chilli in the oil. Add in the garam masala and fry on a low heat for 2 minutes. This can be done in a pan over the BBQ outside or on the hob.

Add in the spring onion and red pepper. Cook for another 2 minutes. Add in the water. Simmer for 3-4 minutes until the pepper softens. Season. Put to one side.

Skewer the prawns onto kebab sticks. Grill or BBQ for two minutes on each side, keep turning the sticks to ensure the prawns are cooked through.

Stir the chopped coriander and 1tbsp natural yoghurt into the red pepper mixture. Season well. Warm the chapatis in the oven or over the fire. Spoon a little mango chutney onto each one. Top with the red pepper mixture. Lay the prawn skewers across the top. Garnish with a little coriander. Drizzle with the 1tbsp reserved yoghurt. Eat!

Turkey Meatballs with Herbs, Peas and Broad Beans

1 slice white bread, crusts removed • 1 tbsp milk • 150g turkey mince • 1 egg • 1 tsp fresh parsley, finely chopped • 1 tsp fresh sage, finely chopped • 2 tbsp oil • Salt and pepper

FOR THE SAUCE:

1 onion, diced • 1 clove garlic, crushed • 300ml chicken stock • 75g bulgur wheat • 1 tin (300g) broad beans drained, or frozen with skin removed • 50g peas • 1 tbsp mint • 1 tbsp parsley • Salt and pepper

Soak the bread in the milk for 10 minutes until soft. In a bowl mix the turkey, bread and milk, egg, parsley, sage and seasoning. Mix really well then form into balls or patties. The mixture will be wet.

Heat the oil in a frying pan and add the meatballs until browned all over (mostly) for 8 to 10 minutes.

Remove from the pan and put to one side. In the pan fry the onion and garlic. Add the stock and bulgur wheat. Simmer for 5 minutes on a low heat.

Add the meatballs back into the pan and simmer for 15 minutes, stirring the meatballs to turn them over every few minutes. Add a little water if it becomes too dry.

Add the broad beans and peas, simmer for 5 minutes then stir in the herbs. Season to taste.

Roasted New Potato Salad with Samphire and Crab

450g new potatoes, cooked • 1 tbsp rapeseed oil • 25g butter • 2 cloves garlic, crushed • ½ red chilli, diced • 50g samphire, rinsed

DRESSING:

150g radishes, trimmed • 1 lime juice and zest • Pinch of sugar • A handful of each chopped: Parsley, Mint, Dill • ½ chilli, diced • Oil

The meat of 1 fresh crab (or 1 tin of crabmeat)

Make the dressing: Slice the radishes and place in a bowl. Stir in the lime juice and zest. Add the sugar, herbs, chilli and oil. Mix well. Put to one side.

Slice the potatoes and fry in the oil and butter with the garlic and chilli. Fry until golden and beginning to crisp. Stir frequently. The garlic will go golden too.

Stir in the samphire and fry, stirring for 3 minutes until the samphire is wilting.

Leave to partially cool then stir into the radishes whilst a little warm.

Leave to cool.

Gently stir in the crabmeat and season with pepper. Add salt if needed, remember that the samphire will be salty.

Serve with a dollop of mayonnaise and crusty bread and butter.

Tomato Tart

PASTRY:

175g plain flour • 75g butter • 1 tsp dijon mustard • 25g grated cheddar • 1 egg yolk

FILLING:

3 tbsp red pesto (see below) • 400g heritage tomatoes - different varieties and colours • 6 olives sliced • Salt and pepper • 1 tbsp olive oil • 2 cloves garlic, finely chopped • 25g cheddar, grated • Basil to garnish • Borage flowers to decorate

PESTO:

1 red pepper • 1 tomato • 1 clove garlic, peeled • 1 tbsp olive oil • 50g walnuts • 1 tbsp walnut oil • 10 basil leaves • 30g mature cheddar • 1 tsp red wine vinegar • Salt and pepper

Roast the pepper, tomato and garlic with the oil at 180C/Fan 160C/ Gas Mark 4 for 20 minutes or until soft.

Toast the nuts in a dry pan.

Put the toasted nuts, pepper, tomato, garlic and walnut oil in a blender. Add the basil and grated cheddar. Blitz until smooth. Stir in the vinegar.

Season to taste.

Turn the oven to 180C/160C Fan/Gas mark 4.

Rub the butter into the flour until it looks like breadcrumbs. Add the mustard and grated cheddar. Stir in the egg yolk and a little water to form a dough. Chill in the fridge for 20 minutes.

Slice the tomatoes.

Roll out the pastry and line a 20cm flan tin. Bake blind for 15 minutes or until slightly golden.

Spread 3 tbsp pesto onto the pastry case base.

Layer the tomatoes in the pastry case sprinkling olives and seasoning between each layer.

Fry the garlic in oil until just crisp. Sprinkle onto the tomatoes with the oil and cheddar. Place back into the oven for 10 to 15 minutes until the tomatoes are just softened and the cheese is melted. Decorate with basil and borage flowers.

Limoncello Tiramisu

100g caster sugar • 4 lemons • 2 tbsp limoncello plus for the mascarpone layer • 500g mascarpone • 500ml double cream • 50g icing sugar • 150g lemon curd • 200g sponge cake cut into fingers • 1 tbsp cocoa

Make a lemon syrup by placing the sugar, juice and rind of three lemons with 50ml water into a pan. Slowly bring to the boil to dissolve the sugar and then simmer until syrupy. About 5 minutes. Remove from the heat. Stir in 2 tbsp limoncello.

Beat together the mascarpone and double cream. Fold in the icing sugar, 100g lemon curd and limoncello to taste. Add the juice and zest of the fourth lemon.

Place half of the sponge fingers into a dish. Drizzle over half of the syrup. Spread half of the cream mixture over the top. Place the remaining sponge fingers on top, drizzle the remaining syrup over the top. Then use the remaining cream to cover over the sponge fingers. Dot with the remaining lemon curd and dust with the cocoa powder.

Place in the fridge for at least two hours.

Raspberry and White Chocolate Cheesecake

250g shortbread biscuits • 100g butter • 200g cream cheese • 250g mascarpone • 150ml double cream • 2 eggs • 150g raspberries • ¼ tsp vanilla essence 150g white chocolate plus a little extra grated for decorating • 50g icing sugar plus extra for dredging

TOPPING:

1 tub of crème fraiche and a punnet of raspberries

Grease a 20cm, 8 inch springform flan tin. Turn the oven to 180C/ Fan 160C/ Gas Mark 4.

Blitz the biscuits in a food processor. Melt the butter. Mix into the biscuits really well and press into the tin so it comes up the sides.

Whisk the cream cheese, mascarpone and cream together until smooth. Beat in the eggs. Stir in the raspberries and essence. Melt the chocolate and stir in with the icing sugar.

Bake for 35 to 40 minutes until it wobbles. Turn off the oven and leave to cool.

Top with crème fraiche piled on top with the raspberries and dredge with icing sugar.

Sprinkle with the white chocolate saved. Chill well before serving.

IT'S
ECKŌ

Peach and Strawberry Roulade with Borage and Basil

25g butter for brushing • 180g caster sugar, plus some for dusting • 100g plain flour • 1 tsp baking powder • 6 eggs, separated • 150ml whipping cream • 150g strawberries • 2 ripe peaches • A handful of Basil leaves • A handful of borage flowers • 25g icing sugar

Heat the oven to 180C/fan 160C/gas 4. Line a 34 × 24cm swiss roll tin or baking tray with baking parchment. Let the parchment come about 1 cm over the sides of the tin. Brush with butter and dust with caster sugar.

Beat the egg yolks and sugar together with electric beaters until very light and thick. Sift in the flour and baking powder and fold in.

Whisk the egg whites until firm and then fold into the cake mix without squashing out too much air.

Spoon into the tin, level the top and bake for 15-20 minutes until golden brown and a skewer comes out clean.

Cool for 10 minutes and then turn out onto another piece of baking parchment dusted with caster sugar. While the cake is still warm, roll it up so it looks like a swiss roll. Cool.

Chop the strawberries and peaches.

Whip the cream until thick.

Unroll the roulade as much as you can – it can be tricky to unroll the very last bit.

Spread the cream over the roulade without getting too close to the edges, it will squash out as it rolls. Dot all over with the strawberries and peaches. Save some to decorate. Place on the basil leaves. Roll up. Top with a little spoonful (or pipe) cream at intervals on the top.

Add on strawberry and peach and a borage flower. Dust with icing sugar.

aut

umn

Ferry Project: our vision for the future

It is a sad truth that there will always be a need for charities like the Ferry Project. Yet by giving each homeless person personalised support, appropriate accommodation, and opportunities to learn and succeed, we can continue to see lives changing and our communities thriving.

Every single one of our clients has faced rejection and failure on their journey into homelessness. Every homeless person has experienced trauma, and many have made poor choices in a desperate attempt to alleviate their pain. They often think little of themselves, and as society rejects them they begin to believe that they are worthless.

We are here to help them rebuild their lives, both inside and out. We believe this can be achieved by giving each person three things:

Personalised support designed for their unique personality and individual circumstances

Value and self esteem by providing beautiful and well considered accommodation

Opportunities to be successful in something, by helping them to find a job, learn a new skill, reconnect with their family, find a new home, improve their physical or mental health, or develop a new hobby

As we build each person up, we can help them to realise that their past mistakes are behind them. They are worthy of love, and as this truth settles deep into their hearts they can move forward and thrive.

As we look ahead to the Ferry Project's future, there is much to be excited about.

We are committed to creating and strengthening more links with local health services and community organisations to improve our clients' health and wellbeing.

We are developing our employment work so that we can give our clients and local residents the best opportunities to develop their skills and find suitable jobs.

We are striving to develop arts & culture in the local area, facilitating cultural activities for the benefit of the whole community.

Finally, we will never cease improving the unique support we give to each and every person who arrives at our door. Every person who moves out of homelessness is worth celebrating, and in the process we will help them to find healing for their trauma, growth for their self esteem, and hope that the future is worth fighting for.

Jubilee Place

Octavia View & Gardens

Ashley's Story

I live with my wonderful mum and dad and have a passion for cooking, so I was thrilled when I found out about the Ferry Project Cookery School. I love cooking as it gives me new skills and makes me feel independent, which is very valuable as someone with Down's Syndrome, and it helps me feel relaxed and calm.

When I cook with all the different meats, vegetables and spices, it's like I'm on Masterchef. Even more so when I wear my chef whites - they make me feel like a proper chef. I like following instructions, and I'm really glad I can get a certificate at the end of the course. No one listens to me like Alison. My favourite dish that I've ever made was Prawn Risotto. It was banging!

In 2024 something amazing happened. Alison and I went to London together and we met Cyrus Todiwala OBE! Cyrus was the best. He made us coffee and showed us around his restaurant and his cookery school. I told him about the Ferry Project, a charity that I love, and about my own cooking journey. It was an amazing day.

My cooking lessons have helped me so much. I'm more independent now, which is good as Mum can't always do everything for me. I love the pictures of me cooking that Alison posts to Facebook. One time I even got the opportunity to help Alison with a live cooking demonstration, chopping and following her instructions.

I have made loads of new friends, and I get really, really excited every time I get to go to the Ferry Project Cookery School!

Ashley meets Cyrus Todiwala

Beetroot Soup with Horseradish Croutons

25g butter • 1 tbsp oil • 1 onion, diced • 2 cloves garlic • 2 potatoes, peeled and diced • 1 carrot, diced • 1 kilo raw beetroot, diced and peeled • 2 tsp horseradish • 1½ litre vegetable stock • 2 sprigs fresh thyme (plus a little for garnish) • 150ml double cream • Salt and pepper

CROUTONS:

½ sourdough loaf cut into cubes • 2 tbsp oil • 2tbsp horseradish • 50ml sour cream.

Melt the butter. Add the oil. Fry the vegetables for 5 minutes, stirring.

Add in the horseradish and stock. Place on a lid. Simmer for 45 minutes until the beetroot is soft.

Add the thyme. Blend until smooth.

Stir in the cream and warm back through. Season well.

Croutons – mix the oil and horseradish. Coat the cubes of bread in the oil mixture. Place on a baking sheet and roast for 10 to 12 minutes at 180C/Gas 4, turning every so often. Serve on top of the soup with a sprig of thyme, and a spoonful of sour cream.

Sausage, Apple and Cheese Pasties

PASTRY:

200g plain flour • Pinch of mustard powder •
100g butter • 50g grated cheddar

FILLING:

1 grated small apple • 4 sausages • 2 rasher cooked bacon • Handful fresh thyme • 2 tbsp chutney •
1 beaten egg for brushing

Turn oven to 180C/ 160C Fan oven/ Gas Mark 4

Sift the flour and mustard powder. Rub in the butter. Stir in the cheddar and enough cold water to form a dough. Leave to rest for 30 minutes.

In a bowl mix together the grated apple, sausage meat, chopped bacon, cheddar and thyme.

Roll out the pastry and cut into circles. Spread a little chutney in the very middle of the circle. Place a little filling on top. Brush some cold water around the edge and bring up the edges to form a pasty. Seal the edges together.

Brush with beaten egg and bake for approximately 25 minutes. This depends on how big your pasties are! Make sure they are 75 degrees C in the centre and the sausage is cooked through.

EGISTER NOW
ACTIVATE YOUR
REE GUARANTEE
00 032 8936
ZANUSSI

Apple and Fennel Salad with Norfolk Cheeses and Bacon

1 fennel bulb • 2 dessert apples • 1 red onion •
Two handfuls of watercress • 50g walnut halves •
4 rashers bacon, cooked to crispy • 75g Binham blue, roughly chopped into chunks (or another blue cheese) •
75g Copys Cloud Cheese, roughly chopped into chunks (or a brie style cheese)

DRESSING:

1 clove garlic • 5 tsps olive oil • 1 tsp cider vinegar •
Pinch salt • 1 tsp mustard

Start with the dressing. Crush the garlic. Beat in the oil, vinegar, salt and mustard. Put to one side.

Thinly slice the fennel across the bulb. Core the apple and slice thinly, leave the skin on. Thinly slice the onion. Mix together. Stir in the watercress. Roughly chop the walnuts and stir in. Crumble the bacon and gently mix through. Add in the Binham Blue and Copys Cloud. Drizzle over the dressing and gently mix being careful not to break up the cheese too much.

Chilli with Black Beans and Eggs

SERVES 4

500g minced beef • 2 onions, diced • 2 cloves garlic, crushed • 1 carrot, diced • 1 red pepper, diced • 1 tsp cumin • 1 tsp paprika • Pinch of chilli flakes according to taste • 2 tbsp tomato puree • 400g tin tomatoes • 1 beef stock cube • 250ml water • 1 small tin red kidney beans • 100g black beans • 4 eggs • 2 tbsp chopped parsley, or 2 tsp dried parsley

Put the mince into the pan and stir well. It will start to brown and release it's own fat. Add the onion, garlic, carrot and pepper.

Fry for 3 minutes until starting to soften. Stir in the spices. Add the tomato puree. Stir in the tinned tomatoes and beef stock cube. Add in the water. Stir well. Leave to simmer for 15 minutes. Check part way through cooking, stir and add a little more water if needed.

Stir in the kidney and black beans.

Make four indentations on the top and break in the eggs. Make sure it is not boiling, just simmering. Place on a lid and cook until the egg is set. Sprinkle with parsley and serve with crusty bread, rice or a jacket potato.

Shepherd's Pie with Cauliflower Mash

200g minced lamb • 1 carrot, diced • 1 onion, diced • 2 garlic cloves, crushed • 1 courgette finely diced • 1 parsnip peeled and finely diced • 1 tbsp tomato puree • 300g green lentils (merchant gourmet puy are good!) • A handful of parsley, chopped finely • 100ml red wine • 300ml lamb stock

CAULIFLOWER MASH:

2 cauliflowers • 1 tbsp olive oil • 2 cloves garlic • Salt and pepper • fresh thyme

Turn oven to 200C/Fan 180C/ Gas Mark 7

Add the lamb to a large pan. Add in the carrot, onion, garlic, courgette, parsnip. Let the fat from the lamb gently sauté the vegetables. Add in the puree, lentils and parsley. Stir in the wine. Simmer for 2 minutes. Add in the stock. Simmer for 30 minutes.

Chop the cauliflower into 5cm chunks. Put into a pan with the garlic peeled and 2 tbsp water. Steam until tender. Add the oil and mash. Season to taste. Stir in some fresh thyme. If it is too sloppy just place over the heat and dry off a little.

Place the lamb mixture into an ovenproof dish. Top with the mash. Bake for 25 minutes or until golden on top.

Pumpkin Curry with Spiced Crispy Rice

2 tbsp rapeseed oil • 1 onion, diced • 1 clove garlic, crushed • 1 red chilli, diced • 1 cm root ginger, diced • 1 carrot, diced • 1 potato, peeled and diced • 500g diced, peeled pumpkin • 1 tsp cumin • 1 tsp ground coriander • 1 tsp garam masala • ½ tsp turmeric • ½ tsp cinnamon • ½ tsp paprika • 100ml vegetable stock • 1 tin chick peas • 1 tin coconut milk • Salt and pepper • Handful of fresh coriander

CRISPY FRIED RICE:

300g cooked cold rice • 50g butter • 1 tbsp oil • A little salt

Heat the oil in a pan. Fry the onion and garlic with the chilli and ginger for 3 minutes. Add the carrot, potato and pumpkin. Fry for 2 minutes. Add the spices and fry on a low heat for 2 minutes. Stir in the vegetable stock. Place on the lid and simmer on a low heat for 10 minutes. The vegetables will cook partially in the water and partially be steamed.

Stir in the chick peas and coconut milk. Warm through.

Using a hand blender blitz very sparingly just to give a background to the curry. Most of the vegetables should remain as chunks. Season to taste. Stir in the coriander and serve with the crispy rice

For the rice: line a frying pan with greaseproof paper. Melt 25g butter on the paper with the oil. Add the rice and stir in the remaining butter. Place a cartouche over the top and cook through until golden and crispy underneath. To look at how the rice is cooking gently lift the paper to peep underneath. It will take about 10 to 15 minutes

Carefully turn in out onto a plate with the crispy side up. Season with salt.

Pear and Ginger Cake

4 pears • 150ml cider • 2 tbsp demerara sugar • 225g butter • 225g light brown sugar • 4 eggs • 275g self raising flour • ½ tsp ground ginger • 2 stem ginger, finely diced • 2 tbsp stem ginger syrup • 4 tbsp demerara sugar for the syrup

Peel, halve and core the pears. Place 3 pears in a pan in the cider and poach for 10 mins until soft. Save the fourth for the cake.

Grease and line a 20cm/8 inch tin. Place the pears in the tin core side upwards. Retain the cider for later.

Turn oven to 180C/Fan 160C/ Gas Mark 4

Cream the butter and sugar. Fold in the eggs. Fold in the flour and ground ginger. Dice the remaining pear and stir into the cake mixture. Stir in the stem ginger and syrup. Pour the cake mixture onto the pears. Bake for 30 to 40 minutes until firm to touch.

Heat the cider with the sugar and slow boil for 3 to 5 minutes to make a syrup.

Remove the cake from the oven. Leave to stand for 10 minutes then turn out so the pears are now the top of the cake. Pour the syrup over the cake.

Delicious warm or cold with a dollop of thick cream or crème fraiche.

Chocolate, Date and Banana Cake

50g dates, chopped • 2 tbsp rum • 125g caster sugar • 2 eggs • 125g salted butter • 50g plain flour • 25g cocoa • 125g plain dark chocolate • 1 small banana, mashed

Turn the oven to 180C/Fan 160C/ Gas Mark 4. Grease and line a 20cm/ 8 inch cake tin.

Soak the dates in the rum for half an hour.

Beat together the sugar and eggs.

Melt the butter and whisk into the egg mixture. Sift in the flour and cocoa.

Melt the chocolate and add to the egg mixture. Stir in the dates and rum. Stir in the banana.

Pour into the cake tin and bake for 30 to 40 minutes.

Turn the oven down to 160C/Fan 140C/Gas Mark 3 and cover with greaseproof if it begins to cook too quickly on the top.

Delicious served hot or cold on it's own or with clotted cream. Or warm with a chocolate sauce made by melting 125g dark chocolate with 75g butter and 50ml double cream.

Really Moist Spice Cake

315g plain flour • 3 tsp baking powder • 1 tsp cinnamon • 1 tsp nutmeg • ¼ tsp ginger • ¼ tsp allspice • 175g butter • 250g caster sugar • 1 egg • 3 egg yolks • 300ml milk • 2 tbsp black treacle

FROSTING:

50g butter • 200g cream cheese • 100g icing sugar • A little stem ginger and syrup

Turn the oven to 180C/Fan 160C/Gas Mark 3. Grease and line a 7 inch, 18cm cake tin.

Sift the flour, baking powder and spices.

In a separate bowl cream together the butter and sugar. Add the egg and egg yolks. Fold in the flour and spices. Stir in the milk and black treacle. Mix well. Pour into the cake tin and bake for 45 to 55 minutes or until firm to touch. Cover with baking parchment if it starts to brown too much on the top. Leave to stand before removing from the tin.

For the frosting beat together the butter, cream cheese and icing sugar. Drizzle in a little stem ginger syrup. Mix well

Once the cake is cold spread on the frosting. Dot with slices of stem ginger.

Almond Croissant and Blackberry Bread and Butter Pudding

6 almond croissants • 60g butter • 300ml double cream • 100ml milk • 3 eggs • 1 tsp almond essence • 3 tbsp caster sugar • 150g blackberries

Slice open the croissants. Spread on the butter. Beat together the cream, milk, eggs and essence.

Place half the croissants butter side up in an ovenproof dish. Sprinkle on the blackberries and 2 tbsp caster sugar. Place on the remaining croissants butter side up. Pour over the egg mixture slowly allowing it to trickle down through the croissants. Sprinkle with the remaining sugar.

Leave to soak for at least an hour, preferably overnight.

Bake at 180C/ Fan 160C/ Gas Mark 4 for 25 to 30 minutes or until set and golden on top.

SLOW COOK

About The Author and The Ferry Project Cookery School

THE FERRY PROJECT COOKERY SCHOOL

Our cookery school is based at Octavia View in Wisbech and is for anyone who wants to learn how to cook, or those wanting to develop their cooking skills.

As part of the Ferry Project, our Cookery School provides vocational skills and work experience in hospitality for our homeless clients, alongside training in useful cooking skills which equip them to live independently. This forms a vital part of the holistic homelessness support we provide to our clients.

Our Cookery School is also a social enterprise, which means that by running classes, courses and events for the general public in our local community, it helps to generate an income for the charity which in turn helps us to continue our work to assist homeless single adults on their journey towards independent living.

ALISON CROUCH

The Cookery School is run by our tutor, Alison Crouch, who has 35 years of experience working in the food industry and is passionate about enabling others to cook. She has managed restaurants, created recipes, presented at food shows alongside Gordon Ramsay and Rosemary Shrager, studied food history while working with the National Trust, and helped people through her magazine articles and radio phone-ins.

COURSES, CAFES AND MORE

There is always a full schedule of events and courses on offer and include things such as community classes, talks and demonstrations, special food events, classes for the elderly and school groups, courses about specific cuisines, food history, opportunities to enhance your culinary skills, cooking workshops, corporate hospitality events, pop-up cafes, group cooking classes, one-on-one sessions and much more.

Please visit our website for details ferryproject.org.uk/cookery-school

Or scan this QR code with your mobile phone:

Ferry Project
COOKERY SCHOOL
FUNDED BY CAMBRIDGESHIRE
COUNTY COUNCIL & ALLISON HOMES.
Opened on 8th November 2024
By The Rt Hon Steve Barclay MP

www.ingramcontent.com/pod-product-compliance
Ingram Content Group UK Ltd.
Pitfield, Milton Keynes, MK11 3LW, UK
UKHW052040120225
454937UK00004B/23
* 9 7 8 1 0 6 8 3 3 2 7 1 5 *